Glam Wedding FLORALS

Your wedding day will truly be your "Best Day Ever" when you know how to get the glam look you want for less. Whether you use fresh flowers or silk, you can make them look fabulous by following the easy steps in this DIY guide.

LEISURE ARTS, INC. • Maumelle, Arkansas

Best Day Ever! Plaque

SHOPPING LIST

- ☐ laser cut wood plaque (ours is about 16" x 22" with a 11" x 15" area for words)
- ☐ black matte spray paint
- ☐ gold metallic acrylic paint
- ☐ 11 white small rosebuds
- ☐ fern bush, cut apart
- ☐ 3 yards of 1½" wide gold wire-edged ribbon
- ☐ gold glitter spray
- ☐ small paintbrush
- ☐ transfer paper
- ☐ dull pencil or stylus
- ☐ 3" diameter floral foam half ball
- ☐ floral wire
- ☐ wire cutters
- ☐ low temp glue gun & glue sticks

To make the Plaque:

1. Spray paint the plaque black. Allow to dry completely.
2. To make a pattern, use a computer to print "Best Day Ever!" in the desired font to fit on your plaque. Use transfer paper and the dull pencil or stylus to transfer the pattern to the plaque.
3. Paint the letters with the gold paint and allow to dry completely.
4. Glue the foam half ball at the top front of the plaque.
5. To make the bow, measure out 12" from one end of the gold ribbon for the tail; gather the ribbon between your fingers. Measure out 12" again, gather, and bring the gathers to meet the first gathered point, forming a loop; hold the gathered points together. Twist the ribbon, measure out 12", gather, and bring the gathers to meet the gathered point, forming a second loop; hold the gathered points together ***(Fig. 1)***. Make 4 more loops in the same manner. Tightly wrap a floral wire length around the gathers to secure the bow. Leave the tails long for now.

Fig. 1

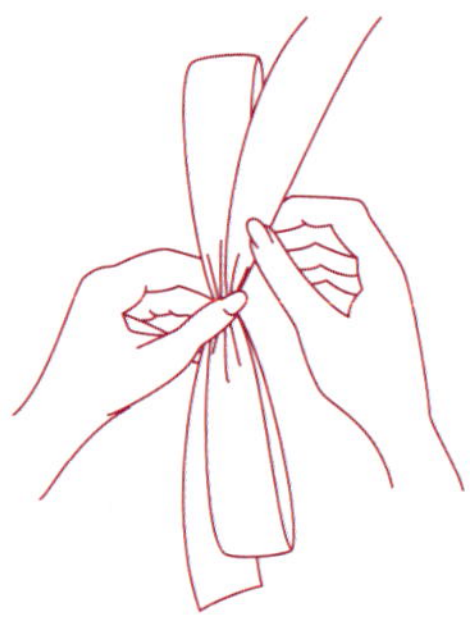

6. Spray the rosebuds and fern fronds with the glitter spray; allow to dry.
7. Insert the fern fronds into the foam, trimming the stems as needed. Trimming each rosebud stem as needed, insert the buds into the foam. Trim the bow wire ends to about 1" and insert into the foam, shaping and trimming the tails as desired. If needed, reinforce the fronds, rosebuds and bow with glue.

Best
day
Ever!

Birdcage Floral

SHOPPING LIST

- ☐ white metal birdcage with crystal bird finial (ours is about 7" diameter & 13" tall)
- ☐ preserved moss
- ☐ small greenery bush
- ☐ white rose stems (2 large & 1 medium)
- ☐ 2 white rosebud stems
- ☐ 6 crystal floral picks
- ☐ 24" of 2" wide pearl-edged white sheer ribbon
- ☐ silver glitter spray
- ☐ floral foam disc or floral foam half ball to fit in birdcage
- ☐ floral pins
- ☐ wire cutters
- ☐ low temp glue gun & glue sticks

To make the Birdcage Floral:

1. Glue the floral foam disc or half ball to the birdcage bottom. Cover the foam with moss, securing with floral pins as necessary.
2. Cut the greenery bush apart and trim the stems to various lengths. Arrange the greenery stems and insert them into the foam, covering the foam completely.
3. Trimming the stems to various lengths, arrange the roses and buds and insert them into the foam. Insert 5 of the crystal picks into the foam.
4. Tie a ribbon bow around the bottom of the bird. Trim and shape the bow tails as desired. Slide the remaining crystal pick through the knot on the bow, trimming the stem if needed. Glue the pick in place.
5. Working on a covered surface, spray the entire design with the glitter spray.

Caution: Never leave burning candles unattended.

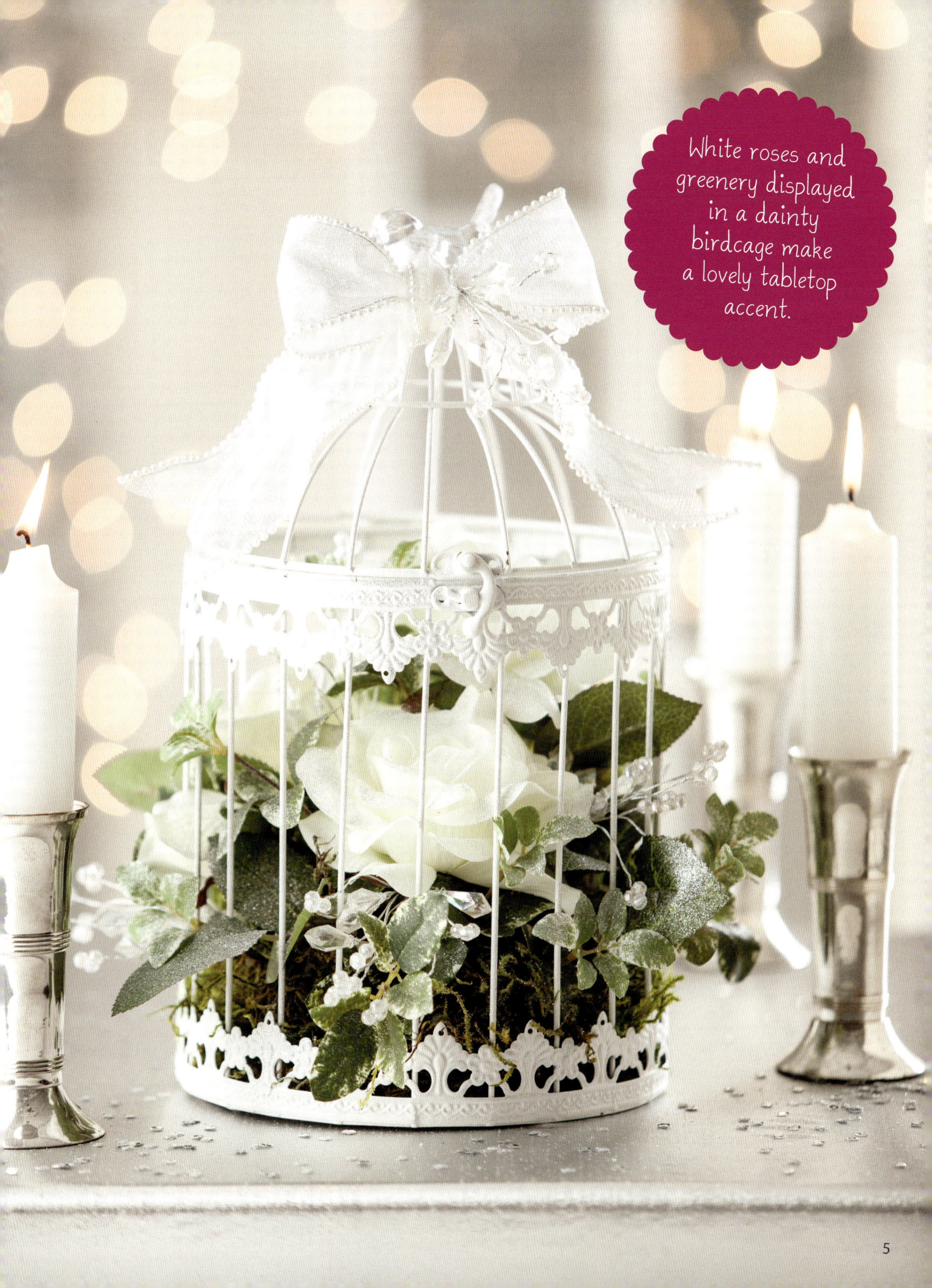
White roses and
greenery displayed
in a dainty
birdcage make
a lovely tabletop
accent.

Golden Tea Party Arrangement

SHOPPING LIST

- ☐ assorted teapots & teacups
- ☐ floral bush with about 5-6 blossoms for each teapot
- ☐ metallic gold spray paint
- ☐ pearl & gemstone cluster sticker for each teapot (found in the scrapbooking department)
- ☐ flower-shaped floating candle for each teacup
- ☐ floral foam

To make the Arrangement:

1. Wash each teapot and teacup; dry well. Spray paint each piece, making sure to paint the teacup interiors; allow to dry.
2. Fill each teapot with floral foam. Trim the floral bush stems to about 3" below the blossoms. Insert the stems into the foam, completely covering the foam. Adhere a sticker to each teapot.
3. Fill each teacup with water and place a candle in the water.

Thrift store finds become gold and glamorous flower vases.

Caution: Never leave burning candles unattended.

Gold Rope-Covered Jar

SHOPPING LIST

- ☐ quart-size canning jar
- ☐ 26 yards of 5mm diameter metallic gold rope
- ☐ 1 yard of 2" wide white pearl-edged satin ribbon
- ☐ glue gun & glue sticks
- ☐ 1$^1/_2$ dozen fresh white roses

To make the Jar:

1. Wrap the jar with the rope, gluing the rope in place as necessary.
2. Tie the ribbon in a bow around the jar mouth. Trim the ends as desired.
3. Trim the rose stems to the desired length and arrange in the jar.

Caution: Never leave burning candles unattended.

Wedding Arch

SHOPPING LIST

- ☐ ready-to-assemble wedding arch
- ☐ 10 yards of 54" wide white tulle
- ☐ two 12 yard rolls of 6" wide gold glitter organza
- ☐ 4 large white ranunculus & bud stems
- ☐ 4 large white rose stems
- ☐ 6 large white hydrangea stems
- ☐ 4 gold berry floral sprays
- ☐ 2 cans of gold metallic spray paint
- ☐ black enamel acrylic paint
- ☐ dark gold metallic acrylic paint
- ☐ paintbrushes
- ☐ 20" x 42" piece of foam core board
- ☐ transfer paper
- ☐ dull pencil or stylus
- ☐ floral wire
- ☐ awl or Phillips screwdriver to poke holes in foam core board
- ☐ craft knife
- ☐ wire cutters
- ☐ clear tape
- ☐ hot glue gun & glue sticks

To make the Wedding Arch Decorations:

1. Use a photocopier to enlarge the banner 1/2 pattern on page 24 as indicated on the pattern, taping the paper pieces together as needed. Cut out the copy paper 1/2 pattern and trace around it onto the foam core board. Rotating the 1/2 pattern, trace again. Use the craft knife to cut out the banner.
2. Spray paint the banner and the assembled wedding arch gold and allow to dry.
3. Paint the "shaded" areas on the banner indicated in grey on the pattern with the dark gold acrylic paint.
4. Use a computer to print "Mr. & Mrs." in the desired font to fit within a 17" x 5" area. Use transfer paper and the dull pencil or stylus to transfer the words to the banner. Paint the letters with black paint.
5. Matching the ends, fold the tulle in half to find the center. With the center at the top of the arch, weave the tulle in and out of the arch's cross (horizontal) bars. Trim the tulle even with the floor or allow it to pool.
6. Make six 6-loop and one 2-loop gold organza bows. To make each bow, measure out 12" from one end of the organza; gather the organza between your fingers. Measure out 12", gather, and bring the gathers to meet the first gathered point, forming a loop; hold the gathered points together. Twist the organza, measure out 12", gather, and bring the gathers to meet the gathered point, forming a second loop; hold the gathered points together ***(see Fig. 1, page 2)***. Make additional loops if needed in the same manner. Tightly wrap a 12" floral wire length around the gathers to secure the bow. Trim the organza ends as desired.
7. Using the awl or screwdriver, punch holes at the top edge of the banner and wire it to the arch. Trimming the stems as necessary, wire and glue the flowers and berries to the arch, overlapping the top edge of the banner. Wire the 2-loop bow to the top of the arch and three 6-loop bows on each side.

Say "I do" underneath a lovely arch adorned with white tulle, gold glitter organza and flowers all in white.

Bright Floral Arrangements

SHOPPING LIST

For the tall vase arrangement:

- ☐ tall glass vase (ours is a $23^1/_2$" tall pilsner vase)
- ☐ white chalk-finish spray paint
- ☐ clear acrylic matte spray sealer
- ☐ 4 green hydrangea stems
- ☐ 2 dark pink hydrangea stems
- ☐ 4 dark pink rose stems
- ☐ 4 peach rosebud stems
- ☐ 4 dark pink ranunculus stems
- ☐ 3 peach ranunculus stems
- ☐ 2 green lilac stems
- ☐ 2 green snowball stems
- ☐ 3 pink peony stems
- ☐ 6" diameter foam ball (or size to rest on vase)
- ☐ wire cutters
- ☐ low temp glue gun & glue sticks

For each wine glass arrangement:

- ☐ wine glass
- ☐ white chalk-finish spray paint
- ☐ clear acrylic matte spray sealer
- ☐ 2 dark pink rose stems
- ☐ 2 peach rosebud stems
- ☐ 1 green lilac stem
- ☐ 1 green snowball stem
- ☐ 2 dark pink ranunculus stems
- ☐ 1 peach ranunculus stem
- ☐ $2^1/_2$" diameter foam ball (or size to rest on glass)
- ☐ wire cutters
- ☐ low temp glue gun & glue sticks

To make the Arrangements:

1. Spray paint the vase and each wine glass white. When dry, spray the vase and each glass with several coats of clear sealer, allowing to dry between each coat.
2. Glue the foam balls in the vase and glasses.
3. Separate the hydrangeas, snowballs and lilacs into smaller pieces. Trim the stem of each flower for the vase arrangement about 2" below the flower head. Trim the stem of each flower for the wine glass arrangements about 1" below the flower head. Add the flowers by inserting the stems into the foam. Begin with the larger flowers, spacing them evenly. Fill in the empty spaces with the medium and then smaller flowers.

Cascading White Topiary

SHOPPING LIST

- ☐ $19^3/_4$" tall x $5^1/_2$" diameter clear glass cylinder vase
- ☐ 3 white cascading stephanotis stems
- ☐ 4 white cascading pearl spray stems
- ☐ 3 white large rose stems
- ☐ 6 white medium rose stems
- ☐ 3 white small rose stems
- ☐ 2 white rosebud stems
- ☐ 20" square of lace fabric
- ☐ 1 yard of $1^1/_2$" wide white satin ribbon
- ☐ decoupage glue
- ☐ 1" foam brush
- ☐ two 6" diameter foam discs
- ☐ wire cutters
- ☐ low temp glue gun & glue sticks

To make the Topiary:

1. Apply the decoupage glue to the vase with the foam brush. Wrap the lace fabric around the vase, trimming the excess overlap at the back and at the top. Smooth the lace fabric around the vase until there are no wrinkles or air bubbles; allow to dry.
2. Stack and glue the foam discs together. Glue the discs to the top of the vase. Wrap the ribbon around the discs to conceal them; glue the ribbon in place.
3. Trim the stephanotis and pearl stems to about 2" below the first flower or pearl. Insert the stephanotis and pearl stems into the discs, arranging them evenly around the discs.
4. Trim the rose and rosebud stems to about 2" below the blossoms. Insert the stems into the discs, starting with the large roses and arranging them evenly around the discs.

Caution: Never leave burning candles unattended.

Lace and pearls accent an all white bouquet for an elegant centerpiece.

Flower Cone

SHOPPING LIST

- ☐ 8 1/2" x 11" sheet of iridescent glitter cardstock
- ☐ 27" length of 7/8" wide satin ribbon in desired color
- ☐ 20" length of 1 1/2" wide white rose/pearl lace trim
- ☐ 12" disposable decorating bag (found in the cake decorating department)
- ☐ desired fresh flower stems
- ☐ 1/4" hole punch
- ☐ stapler & staples
- ☐ glue gun & glue sticks

To make the Cone:

1. Roll the cardstock into a cone shape; glue in place.
2. For the hanger, punch a hole at each side of the cone. With the ends on the inside of the cone, thread the lace trim through the holes and glue in place.
3. For the bow, punch two holes in the front of the cone about 1" apart. Thread the ribbon through the holes and tie into a bow. Trim the ribbon ends as desired.
4. Trim the decorating bag along the top edge to fit in the cardstock cone. Staple the bag to the cone back, making sure to only staple through the back layer of the bag.
5. Hang the cone. Carefully pour a small amount of water into the decorating bag and add the flowers.

Glittery Bubble Ball Vases

SHOPPING LIST

- ☐ two 5" diameter (at widest point) clear glass bubble ball vases
- ☐ 8" diameter (at widest point) clear glass bubble ball vase
- ☐ pink & dark pink peony floral bushes (enough for a total of about 24 blossoms)
- ☐ four 42 oz. bags of decorative glass gems vase filler
- ☐ gold chunky glitter
- ☐ disposable plate
- ☐ spray adhesive
- ☐ painter's tape
- ☐ wire cutters

To make the Vases:

1. For each vase, wrap painter's tape around the vase about 2" from the top. Working over a covered surface, apply spray adhesive above the tape. Working over the disposable plate to catch the excess, shake the glitter onto the vase. Remove the tape and allow to dry.
2. Fill the vases with the glass gems, using two bags for the larger vase. Cut each blossom stem from the bushes about 4" below the blossom. Place about 12 flowers in the larger vase and 6 in each of the smaller vases, pushing the stems down into the glass gems so that the blossoms are resting on the vase rim.

Caution: Never leave burning candles unattended.

Glittery Gerberas

SHOPPING LIST

- ☐ 3 colored soda bottles
- ☐ 3 white long stem gerbera daisies
- ☐ 1 yard of 1 1/4" wide bling "ribbon"
- ☐ silver chunky glitter
- ☐ scrap of white felt
- ☐ three 12mm clear acrylic gemstones
- ☐ twenty-four 8mm clear acrylic gemstones
- ☐ 24" length of 2" wide sheer ribbon to match soda bottles
- ☐ spray adhesive
- ☐ disposable plate
- ☐ hot glue gun & glue sticks

To make the Gerberas:

1. Hot glue the bottles together. Cut the bling "ribbon" into two 18" lengths. Wrap one bling length around the bottle grouping near the bottom; glue the bling in place. Repeat with the remaining bling length about 1 1/2" above the first length.
2. Tie a sheer ribbon bow around one bottle. Trim the ribbon ends as desired.
3. For each flower center, cut a 1" diameter felt circle. Glue a 12mm gemstone to the circle center. Glue eight 8mm gemstones around the center stone. Glue the flower center to a gerbera daisy center.
4. Working over a covered surface, apply spray adhesive to one gerbera daisy stem. Working over the disposable plate to catch the excess, shake the glitter onto the stem. Repeat for each stem. When dry, place a stem in each bottle.

Caution: Never leave burning candles unattended.

What a fun way to decorate for the celebration! Coat the long stems in lots of glitter and let the party begin.

Gold Bottles & Candles

SHOPPING LIST

- ☐ assorted clean glass bottles (new and/or used)
- ☐ large ivory long stem roses or ranunculus, some with buds (one for each bottle)
- ☐ $^{3}/_{4}$" wide ivory/gold brocade ribbon (about 5" for each bottle)
- ☐ gold chunky glitter
- ☐ glass votive holders
- ☐ votive candles (one for each holder)
- ☐ metallic gold spray paint
- ☐ gold glitter spray
- ☐ spray adhesive
- ☐ wire cutters
- ☐ glue gun & glue sticks
- ☐ disposable plate

To make the Bottles & Candles:

1. Spray paint each bottle metallic gold; allow to dry. Wrap a brocade ribbon length around each bottle neck; glue in place.
2. Working over a covered surface, spray each flower (including the leaves) with glitter spray. Allow to dry. Place a flower stem in each bottle, trimming the stems to different heights.
3. Working over the covered surface, apply spray adhesive to a votive holder. Working over the disposable plate to catch the excess, shake the glitter onto the votive holder. Repeat for each votive holder. When dry, place a candle in each holder.

Caution: Never leave burning candles unattended.

Heart Wreath

SHOPPING LIST

- ☐ pre-made 8" wide boxwood wreath
- ☐ 7 white rosebud stems
- ☐ 17" length of 1 1/2" wide grosgrain ribbon in desired color
- ☐ floral wire
- ☐ wire cutters
- ☐ low temp glue gun & glue sticks

To make the Wreath:

1. If the wreath has a hanger on the back, carefully remove it.
2. For the ribbon hanger, cut a 10" length of wire. Fold the ribbon length in half and gather the ends. Tightly wrap the gathered ends with the wire length. Twist the wire ends together and insert into the hole created when you removed the hanger. Fill the hole with glue to secure the ribbon hanger. If there is not a hole from removing the hanger in Step 1, insert the twisted wire into the wreath back and secure with glue.
3. Trim the rosebud stems to about 1/2" below the buds. Glue the rosebuds to the wreath.

Hydrangeas on a Stand

SHOPPING LIST

- ☐ 6 large purple hydrangea stems
- ☐ glass candlestick about 12" tall (we found ours at a thrift store)
- ☐ glass plate about 12" diameter
  ***Note:** Our plate has a pierced edge and we wove $1^1/_2$" wide white satin ribbon through the piercings.*
- ☐ pink chalk-finish spray paint
- ☐ clear acrylic matte spray sealer
- ☐ 4" diameter floral foam half ball
- ☐ E6000® industrial strength adhesive
- ☐ low temp glue gun & glue sticks

To make the Arrangement:

1. For the stand, use E6000 to adhere the plate on the candlestick; allow to dry. Spray paint the stand pink and allow to dry. Apply several coats of spray sealer, allowing to dry between each coat.
2. With glue gun, glue the foam half ball to the stand center.
3. Trim one hydrangea stem to 3" below the flower head and insert it into the foam half ball at the top center. Trim the remaining hydrangea stems to $2^1/_2$" and insert them around the foam half ball, completely covering the foam.

Rose Wine Glasses

SHOPPING LIST

For each wine glass:

- ☐ plastic wine glass
- ☐ pre-made rose bouquet with about 11 roses
- ☐ acrylic crystal decorative filler mini pebbles
- ☐ metallic gold spray paint
- ☐ painter's tape

To make each Wine Glass:

1. Wrap painter's tape around the wine glass about 3" from the top edge. Spray the glass gold below the tape; remove the tape and allow to dry.
2. Trim the bouquet stem(s) so that the roses will sit at the top of the wine glass. Place the roses in the glass. Fill the glass with the crystal filler pebbles.

Silver Glitter Vases

SHOPPING LIST

For each vase:

- ☐ 5" diameter glass vase
- ☐ grey spray paint
- ☐ spray adhesive
- ☐ silver chunky glitter
- ☐ 12" of $1^1/_2$" black sheer ribbon
- ☐ 1 dozen fresh red roses
- ☐ disposable plate

To make each Vase:

1. Spray paint the vase grey and allow to dry. Working over a covered surface, apply spray adhesive to the vase. Working over the disposable plate to catch the excess, shake the glitter onto the vase. Allow to dry.
2. Tie a ribbon bow around the vase.
3. Trim the rose stems to the desired length and arrange in the vase.

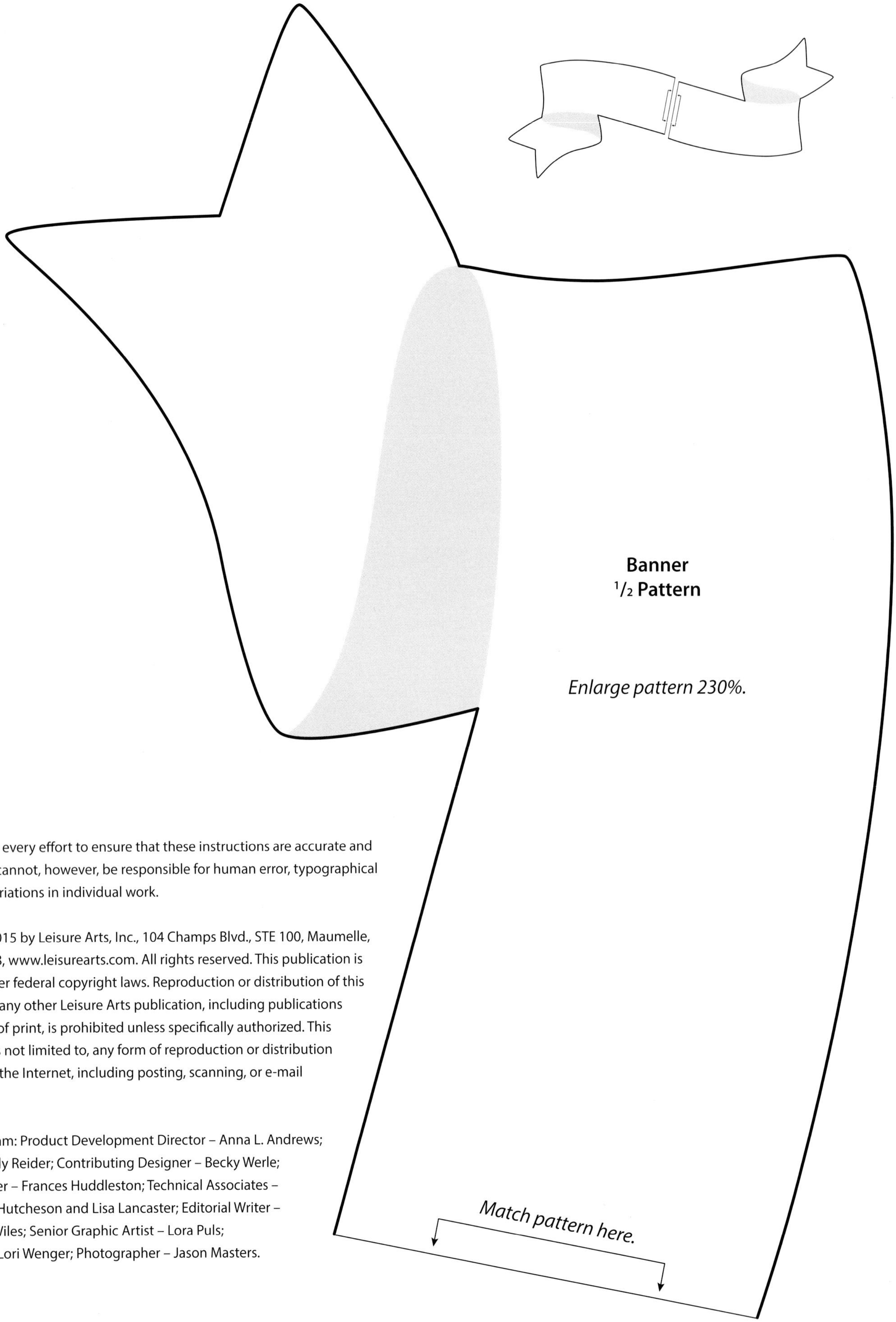

Production Team: Product Development Director – Anna L. Andrews; Designer – Kelly Reider; Contributing Designer – Becky Werle; Technical Writer – Frances Huddleston; Technical Associates – Mary Sullivan Hutcheson and Lisa Lancaster; Editorial Writer – Susan Frantz Wiles; Senior Graphic Artist – Lora Puls; Photostylist – Lori Wenger; Photographer – Jason Masters.